THE
APP FACTORY
PLAYBOOK

How You Can Develop Your App Idea
Without Learning to Code and Without
a Technical Co-Founder

DREW GORHAM

LIONCREST
PUBLISHING

THE APP FACTORY PLAYBOOK

How You Can Develop Your App Idea Without Learning to Code and Without a Technical Co-Founder

ISBN   978-1-61961-691-2 *Paperback*

       978-1-61961-692-9 *Ebook*

THE APP FACTORY PLAYBOOK

To Daphne

CONTENTS

INTRODUCTION

All apps start with an idea; an idea that will help change an industry, fill a void, or alter the way people communicate. The idea is everything when it comes to app creation, but as we know, there are also many steps and a great deal of work between idea phase and finished product.

"Ideas are cheap, execution is everything," says Chris Sacca, early-stage investor in companies like Twitter, Uber, Instagram, Twilio, and Kickstarter. There's truth in this statement, but I prefer Derek Sivers' take: "Ideas are a multiplier of execution." Sivers knows what he's talking about; he wrote an outstanding book called Anything You Want: 40 Lessons for a New Kind of Entrepreneur, based on his experiences starting a company called CD Baby and later selling it for $22 million.

Ideas are just a multiplier of execution

It's so funny when I hear people being so protective of ideas. (People who want me to sign an NDA to tell me the simplest idea.) To me, ideas are worth nothing unless executed. They are just a multiplier. Execution is worth millions:

Awful idea =	-1	No execution =	$1
Weak idea =	1	Weak execution =	$1,000
So-so idea =	5	So-so execution =	$10,000
Good idea =	10	Good execution =	$100,000
Great idea =	15	Great execution =	$1,000,000
Brilliant idea =	20	Brilliant execution =	$10,000,000

To make a business, you need to multiply the two.
The most brilliant idea, with no execution, is worth $20.
The most brilliant idea takes great execution to be worth $20,000,000.
That's why I don't want to hear people's ideas.
I'm not interested until I see their execution. **Derek Sivers** (sivers.org)
Originally posted on Oreillynet.com, August 16, 2005

Startups have two failure modes: not making something, and not making something people want. Both are more common than they should be. This book will help you avoid the first failure mode—not making something.

As an entrepreneur, your idea could result in the next industry-changing app. But without the technical expertise, what resides in the vast space between idea and app can be elusive and scary.

I once worked with a woman with a brilliant idea to revolutionize the world of senior care assisted living. It was her first time developing software, so she contracted a team in India that she found online. They said they could finish it in three months. A year later, with $60,000 less in her bank account, all she had to show for it was a bunch of spaghetti code and no working product.

These stories are incredibly common. The good news is, they're easier to avoid if you know what you're doing.

WHAT THIS BOOK DOES

This book will show you how to outsource the technical expertise to what I call a "rock star freelancer." These are the top 3 percent of software developers worldwide who are ready and willing to build your product vision (often for half the price of an American developer).

WHAT THIS BOOK DOESN'T DO

I'm here to help you take your app to the top through proven design and development techniques and the careful selection of a technical expert. What I can't do is tell you whether your idea is marketable.

How good IS your app idea? Only your customers can tell you whether your idea is good or bad. If you haven't already validated your idea with customers, put this book down and Google "Steve Blank Customer Development."

Steve revolutionized the startup world as one of the

co-inventors of the lean startup movement. He's also built four companies from idea to initial public offering, an achievement only a handful of people in the world can claim. Steve's framework will show you how to stress test your app idea by talking to real customers and make sure your app has potential as a business. If you're interested in learning more, watch these videos (twenty minutes total) and check out the Startup Owner's Manual: appfactorysf. com/resources.

LAUNCH

If you're ready to begin, however, I'll show you how to find and manage the rock stars who can take you from idea to execution, while using the latest tools and design tactics to ensure project success. I recommend you start down the path to success by doing these three things:

- Minimize Risk. Starting a new business is risky enough. In this book, I'll show you how to guarantee you avoid outsourcing horror stories. Most outsourcing projects fail for stupid reasons. Avoiding failure is easy if you know what to do.
- Minimize Price. Great software developers are in high demand and they value their time. By tapping into the global supply, you can work with extremely talented people for below market rates.

- Maximize Speed. Time is money and execution in the startup world means moving fast. Doing the planning and pre-work in this book will save you hundreds of hours of headaches once development begins.

This is the path I've honed building over a hundred apps, from e-commerce and enterprise apps to utility and social media apps. I've worked on projects for established companies like Intel and Tesla, and developed apps for new businesses like Abode (goabode.com), which uses an app to control Abode's home security system and connected devices in the home (security cameras, motion sensors, door locks, lights). Here, I share the path I have followed, and follow to this day, with my customers at App Factory.

Countless books have been written about the process of building an app and the core theme of these books is the same: how to build apps using your technical expertise. What this means, plainly, is that most of the books in circulation are geared toward the coders and software builders, and there are few resources out there for the idea people.

This seems odd to me. There are so many entrepreneurs who don't have a strong technical background, yet they have the customer knowledge and the hustle to launch a successful product, if there were only a more intuitive resource to assist with the technical side of app creation.

My intention with this book is to tailor the app-building process specifically to non-technical people. Much of the conventional knowledge out there will lead you astray and could potentially result in you wasting a lot of valuable time and money.

Why should you listen to me? The lessons in this book were hard-won through my experiences developing one hundred apps over a four-year period. There were many failures and I hope the advice here will help you avoid the mistakes I made along the way.

I started out as a non-technical college graduate who majored in philosophy and graduated with few real-world skills. During my first summer out of college, I helped start a futuristic startup incubator called Singularity University (SU). SU was founded by Ray Kurzweil, Peter Diamandis, and Google co-founder Larry Page to attract the best and brightest entrepreneurs and scientists from around the world to work on massive global problems using exponentially advancing technologies. Watching one hundred entrepreneurs from forty-two countries all working together to build disruptive companies had a profound effect on me. (A *disruptive* innovation is one that creates a new market and value network.)

After a summer immersed in cutting-edge technology

development, I was set on breaking into this alluring startup world.

HOW HARD COULD IT BE?

My plan? Step 1, teach myself how to code. Step 2, build apps for startups.

Coding bootcamps didn't exist back in 2010, so I had to create my own. A friend at SU told me about this program through Harvard Extension where you take classes with Harvard and MIT professors. The classes were cheap and there was no admission requirement to meet, so I flew to Boston and started on the path to becoming a software developer. Most of the Harvard classes were online, so after the first semester I moved back to California and got a job at a software development agency called App Matrix right as the app gold rush was ramping up.

At App Matrix, we built apps for all sorts of clients, from Intel to the cupcake shop down the street. I soon realized two things: First, it takes a lot of work and experience to become a great software developer. Second, I was a much better designer than I was a developer. So instead of spending four years growing from amateur developer to mediocre developer, I decided to focus on product design and project management.

Soon, I was working directly with clients, translating their app ideas into product designs and managing teams of developers to execute the vision. In 2013, I joined another agency called Appstem in San Francisco, the startup mecca. At Appstem, I built apps for Tesla Motors, Enterprise Rent-a-Car, and countless startups. My first experience managing a 100 percent remote team was at Appstem. Our developers were scattered across California and our only workspace was a small room we rented inside an accountant's office in downtown San Francisco. That's where the founder, Robert Armstrong, and I sat.

To my surprise, despite being completely separated from the developers, our team's productivity and quality rose far beyond anything I'd seen before. That was the moment I began to question my default skepticism of outsourcing. The remote developers were happier, more productive, and communicating more clearly, which made my job as project manager much easier. One of our developers would go river surfing when he wasn't coding—not something you can do in a conventional office setting.

Often, we'd get to work with a non-technical startup founder who had the next big app idea. These were my favorite projects. Taking big risks on big ideas was a thrill. In fact, it was so thrilling that I decided to start my own development agency focused specifically on these types of projects. I called it App Factory.

Part of the reason I moved to San Francisco was to immerse myself in a culture filled with technical talent. When I started App Factory, I naturally looked for developers in my own backyard. I had moderate success finding developers on Craigslist and LinkedIn, but they were expensive. In San Francisco, $2,000 per week gets you a newbie developer.

I was constantly experimenting with new ways to build software—new tools, fresh designs, breakthrough project management tactics. One day, I saw a TechCrunch article titled "The Biggest Startup No One Talks About," featuring the company Toptal. Toptal is a freelance engineer marketplace where all the engineers are meticulously vetted through a highly rigorous screening process. Only 3 percent make it through. Their core function is to find the needle in the haystack. At the same time, Toptal vets the projects that are allowed onto the platform. They protect employers and developers. Luckily, the development and design tactics I learned over the years made my projects appealing to developers on the Toptal platform.

The first Toptal developer I had the pleasure of working with was Ivan from Zagreb, Croatia. Croatia has a youth unemployment problem, so many young people loaded up on graduate school and are now looking for work. Ivan is one of the most intelligent, professional developers I've ever met. He has a master's degree in computer science and is one of the best Ruby on Rails developers in the world. Ivan likes working with American startups and enjoys the flexibility of working close to home so he can spend time with his wife and kids. He also enjoys a massive cost of living arbitrage opportunity. In 2016, a one-bedroom apartment in the heart of Zagreb costs $300/month, while a one-bedroom in San Francisco's city center runs at least $3,000/month.

Working with Ivan blew me away. It was like riding a bicycle built for two with Lance Armstrong (in the steroid days). The project I expected to take fourteen weeks was finished in five. There was little-to-no debugging and the designs were built according to the specifications. Ivan said it was the best project he'd ever worked on! I trust he doesn't say that to all his project managers.

Since then, I've worked with Toptal developers for all my projects and consistently achieved the same outstanding speed and quality. Without Toptal, this book would not be possible. It's simply too risky to try to vet developers without having a deep technical background yourself. Toptal solves this problem.

If you'd like to work with Toptal for your next project, sign up with this link and contact me at drew@appfactorysf.com for a $1,000 rebate off your first project. They're worth it! https://www.toptal.com/#snag-just-top-coders-today

Through my experiences at App Factory and beyond, I've streamlined a new app-building methodology that provides the most efficient, collaborative, and cost-effective way to get from idea phase to finished product for the non-coders of the world.

Pulling best practices from all my experiences, I aim to guide you through the steps of building your own app, and steer you away from the mistakes many first-time company founders are susceptible to.

Expense aside—we'll come back to ways to get good value for your money—you can't effectively do this alone. You are going to need teammates. To choose those teammates wisely, it pays to consider what value each team member, including you, brings to the table.

THE DREAM TEAM

Rei Inamoto, chief creative officer at AKQA, offered this advice about hiring better teams: "To run an efficient team, you only need three people: a Hipster, a Hacker, and a Hustler." Inamoto's idea about seeking these three archetypes to balance your team has spread widely since he first introduced it at the South by Southwest (SXSW) Conference in 2012. That's because it works. Here's what the ideal team looks like:

- The Hustler: the classic type-A, outgoing sales personality, who understands how to market, develop partnerships, and sell the product.
- The Hacker: the nerdy computer engineer who has genius coding skills and is a wizard at using the latest technologies to build things that were formerly thought of as impossible.
- The Hipster: the designer who can easily translate a big idea into a simple, intuitive, beautiful interface for the end user.

Sometimes there's crossover in these roles, but these jobs need to get done. You can try to do them all yourself, or delegate to experts. The answer is probably a little of both. In this book, I'll show you how to find great hackers and hipsters around the world without leaving your house. If all three boxes are checked, you have the perfect founding team. This framework also maps nicely into the three essential parts of product development explained to me by Carlos González de Villaumbrosia, founder and CEO of Product School, a product manager bootcamp with locations throughout the US.

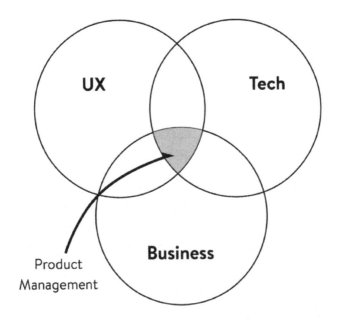

Back in our everyday reality, most situations are far from perfect. Often, people will have the hustler role locked down. Most people reading this book are hustlers. This might be you if you have a domain expertise and a revolutionary idea, but you're missing the technical and design expertise needed to bring that idea to life.

So many remarkable ideas are trapped inside the minds of non-technical founders who have that light bulb moment, but lack connections to the technical people who can implement their concept.

Non-technical co-founders nurture relationships with their

customers and understand their pains, wants, and needs. An on-target app idea develops from this understanding. The co-founders possess the inherent business expertise to market and sell the idea to the intended customer.

Customer development is essential to building a successful business, but the product development component is equally important, which is why, as the non-technical entrepreneur, you need a technical counterpart. You want to be able to get something into the hands of customers as soon as possible. Technology moves quickly, so you need to be fast, too. There's a "first-mover" advantage to those tech companies that put themselves on the market first and establish themselves as leaders in the space.

SO, YOU'RE THE IDEA PERSON. WHAT'S NEXT?

The conventional wisdom of Silicon Valley—the driving force behind that archetypal dream startup team—is that you need a technical co-founder to build a great product. The technical co-founder is, of course, that hacker archetype who finds the intersection between the idea and reality. In other words, hackers are the people who bring products to fruition.

The hustler and the hacker need each other to succeed, but the ugly truth is, there are a whole lot of hustlers in the world and a huge shortage of hackers to fill the technical co-founder role.

Finding this technical yin to your business-savvy yang is essentially like finding and marrying your perfect soul mate. I started a company and have been through a divorce—or I guess I would call it more of an annulment—with my technical co-founder.

Take it from me, working with a technical co-founder is a very serious commitment and should not be rushed into. You need to know your co-founder and rack up years of experience and solid rapport before you tie the knot. A shotgun Vegas wedding just won't cut it.

The truth is, if you go searching for a technical co-founder, you will end up working with the wrong person almost every time.

As a non-technical person, it's extremely difficult to pinpoint the skills you need for your company and verify the technical skillsets of potential co-founders. Even if you can successfully assess a technical partner, the skills you need today might be entirely different than what you will need a few months down the road. Technologies change quickly and as your company grows, so do your technical needs.

All this aside, do you know what the real problem is here? By hiring a technical co-founder, you're giving away half your company to someone you probably don't know too well.

Now that just sounds absurd, doesn't it?

The current Silicon Valley myth that you must have a technical co-founder is only one way to look at developing your team. When you consider all the factors discussed above, this "must have" theory begins to unravel. There are other ways.

One alternative for a non-technical founder is to learn how to code. Plenty of coding websites make it seem like all you have to do is log on and in four weeks BAM! you'll be able to build a functioning web app. It sounds too good to be true, right? Well, that's because it is.

Coding is simply not for everybody, and even if you happen to catch on quickly, it takes a long time to master the skills. We're talking at least six months to two years of full-time study before you'd be ready to create a real, working app product.

The funny thing is, even if you did teach yourself how to code, the end goal would be to transition away from software development when the app gains traction. Ultimately, I believe in leveraging your existing strengths as a non-technical founder rather than spending an extensive amount of time trying to become a mediocre software developer.

Your time would be better spent earning money doing what you already excel at and then hiring an expert for the product development component. From a purely economic standpoint, this is a much more efficient use of your time and resources.

This brings us to another option for non-technical founders who want to build an app: hiring a development agency.

Many avoid this option because the agency fee structure alone is often a budget-breaker for early-stage entrepreneurs. Many agencies charge $6,000 to $20,000 per week to work with them.

Another reason to be wary of agency help is that agencies have incentives that don't align with the entrepreneur's needs. The agency's goal is to maximize the budget of the project so they can generate more revenue. This perspective can result in the agency pushing for additional product features—many of which are unnecessary— so they can profit from the additional time spent. An early-stage founder needs to budget carefully, not be bamboozled into features and designs they don't even need.

I come from the agency world, so I know the pitfalls of this model. In the beginning, clients work with a salesperson who determines the scope of the project. Most of the time, the salesperson doesn't even have the technical background needed to fully understand the timeline and budget for the features they're selling you. That's red flag number one.

Then, during app development, agencies tend to protect their intellectual property, their process, and their developers, which means they don't allow clients to interact with their developers. This results in the app being created in a black box, far removed from the founder. Here, we raise red flag number two.

Agencies tend to use a flawed process that leads to projects that continuously miss deadlines and final products that rarely align with the original vision. Sadly, I've seen many cases where people end up throwing away the work, which is a huge waste of time and money.

The end product emerging from an agency-controlled development process rarely meets expectations because the model is broken.

The founder needs to be involved in the creation process and work closely with the developer. Hundreds of micro-decisions pop up daily; with an agency, the client delegates responsibility and trusts the agency to make the right decisions. As the founder, you're cut out of the creation process and miss out on a huge learning opportunity. In the end, you will still know nothing about product development.

Over the past four years, I've used all three of these approaches. I hired my own technical co-founder, I worked in the agency world, and I even taught myself basic coding. (After a year and a half, however, my knowledge equals only about 10 percent of an experienced developer's wisdom, which goes to show the time and commitment needed to learn how to code.)

The model is broken. Let's go around it.

I know firsthand the strengths and weaknesses of each one of the three traditional app-building approaches. As a result, I started App Factory, which specifically focused on how to meet the needs of early-stage, non-technical founders.

Through App Factory, I built a model that utilizes the best practices from all the approaches, eliminates the time- and money-wasting elements, and, most importantly, allows

the non-technical founder to be an integral part of the app-building process.

App Factory began with a development agency model; we offered an equity discount exchange option. The startups we worked with gave us equity and we provided a lifetime discount on our services in exchange. This model was designed to align incentives better, so that we had vested interest in our clients and operated more as a co-founding partner, rather than just a hired gun.

We operated under this model on our first four or five projects. I realized, though, that we were still developing the apps using the black box approach. Yes, the founders we worked with delivered a high-functioning, impeccably designed, bug-free product, but our clients weren't learning much throughout the process. They were simply outsourcing the development to us and, in the end, became increasingly reliant on us.

My idea for avoiding the problems inherent in the agency model had come back to haunt me. With that in mind, I decided to write this book. I wanted to "open source" all the lessons and best practices developed at App Factory so you can do it yourself.

It's better to teach a man to fish, rather than simply giving

him a fish. As such, my role has shifted from project manager to product mentor and consultant.

I teach clients how to find a good developer and how to avoid the charlatans out there. I train them to be effective and efficient project managers, and guide them step-by-step through their project to maximize their time and effort.

Perhaps most importantly, the App Factory process allows you to build an app without spending hundreds of thousands of dollars.

The App Factory approach to development is an efficient, on-demand model. Rather than hiring an employee—who you must pay regularly, regardless of how much funding is available—you will have the flexibility to engage with them when they are needed, and then turn the tap off when they're not.

App Factory's streamlined process is 50 to 70 percent cheaper than working with an agency and ten times faster than teaching yourself how to code.

My approach, and this book, is designed for you: the non-technical entrepreneur. You are the idea person and you should be in control of how that idea manifests itself in the world. My model and the steps I will describe in the following chapters will help you to take charge and confidently enter the app world. No coding skills necessary.

TALK TO CUSTOMERS FIRST

Let me say this straight out of the gate: not everything can be outsourced. To get the maximum value out of your app, you need to be the world's leading expert when it comes to your users. Where can you reach them? What problem of theirs are you trying to solve? How are they currently solving their problem?

I haven't found a way to outsource this. No one can do this job but you, the entrepreneur.

For those of you using your app to solve your own problem, congratulations. You are your own user. Now all you need to do is find out how many other "yous" are out there.

For the rest of you, it's time to get out of the building and go talk to users.

Talking to users is the most important and the most overlooked part of developing a great app. Trust me, I know how brutal the despair and disappointment can be after you've worked months building your app, only to realize no one wants it. Don't let that happen to you!

In fact, this problem of building a product before talking to users is so pervasive that it sparked a paradigm shift in the startup world called the "lean startup" movement. Started by Steve Blank in the mid-2000s, lean startup assumes that no business plan survives the first contact with customers. Therefore, it's better to talk to customers first, before investing time and money in building a product.

A full exposition of the lean startup process is beyond the scope of this book, but these are the three main components of its methodology:

- Customer Discovery: get outside the building and go talk to customers to discover their habits and pain points.
- Agile Engineering: developing your product iteratively in two-week sprints instead of six-month marathons.
- Minimum Viable Products (MVP): building just enough

features to gather validated learning about your product and customers.

I've seen many instances where founders rushed to build an app without knowing they were totally wrong about their customers. I worked on a project just last year that fell prey to this fallacy. The vision seemed clear during the initial stages: the founders wanted to create an app allowing you to meet new friends in your direct area. The two founders were from Germany. Living in the Bay Area, they noticed a problem. Thousands of international people come to the San Francisco area for work. Living in a new city in a new country, these transplants were struggling to meet new people. Their light bulb moment happened when they realized they could develop an app that would help them connect to the social scene and meet new friends.

Their app offered a way for people to host their own mini-events that others could join. For example, you could post something along the lines of, "Will be playing Frisbee in the park on Saturday, 2:00 p.m. Whoever wants to join me, come on down."

They originally called the app Four & Me because the group was limited to four people, and yourself. If I were to create the event, four other people could RSVP, we would meet up at the park, and maybe we would become friends.

The founding team didn't believe they needed to conduct research, since they themselves were the target customer. They knew the problem that they were trying to solve firsthand and believed if they simply built and launched the app, it would be successful. They didn't even test the idea outside of their own friends and family, most of whom lived in Germany. This was hardly the optimal focus group, because they couldn't provide feedback applicable to an app designed for San Francisco.

We built the app. It worked great. No one signed up. Initially, they received about eighty sign-ups, but seventy of those were friends and family in Germany.

To promote the app, the founding duo rented a booth at Launch Festival, one of the biggest startup launch events in the country. Because they were now interacting with and soliciting feedback from their customers at this event, they received a ton of really useful—and some very critical—feedback that altered their whole product vision.

By talking with their customers, they realized they missed a huge opportunity to create a better product. They should never have skipped the pre-market research. They admitted soliciting feedback from their intended audience should have been the first step, rather than the last. Early feedback would have allowed them to refine the app before wasting their initial investment.

In the end, the founders pivoted their vision, changed their name to Meetly, and positioned themselves as a micro meet-ups app. They developed this term, micro meet-ups, to describe the small, five-person meet-ups the app offered. Their new message was in the customer's language, which they were only able to curate from going out and talking to potential users.

Here's the other thing: It's not enough to just know your users. You also need to know where to find them. Part of being an expert when it comes to your customers is knowing how to reach them. This was another failure of the Four & Me app; they had no idea how to attract users because they didn't know how to reach them.

HOW TO BECOME A USER EXPERT

Perhaps the best resource on how to talk to users is a guy named Giff Constable, author of the book Talking to Humans. Giff's book provides an entertaining and informative guide that shows you the right way to talk to users. You can learn more here: appfactorysf.com/resources.

Here are Giff's tips on running your first customer interviews:

- Talk to one person at a time.
- Know your goals and questions ahead of time.
- Separate behavior and feedback in discussion.
- Get psyched to hear things you don't want to hear.
- Disarm "politeness" training.
- Ask open-ended questions.
- Focus on actual behavior, not speculative or abstract feelings.
- Listen, don't talk.
- Follow your nose and drill down.
- Parrot back or misrepresent to confirm.
- Ask for introductions.
- Write up your notes as quickly as possible.
- Afterward, look for patterns and apply judgment.

Customer development interviews will not give you statistically significant data, but they will give you insights based on patterns. They can be very tricky to interpret, because what people say is not always what they do.

You need to use your judgment to read between the lines, read body language, try to understand context and agendas, and filter out biases based on the types of people in your pool of interviewees. But it is exactly the ability to use human judgment based on human connections that make interviews so much more useful than surveys.

Ultimately, you are better off moving fast and making decisions from credible patterns than dithering about in analysis paralysis.[1]

But you might be saying to yourself, "Great, but how do I find users to talk to?"

Check out Jason Evanish's excellent blog post, "95 Ways to find your first customers for customer development or your first sale." (Find the direct link on appfactorysf. com/resources.)

Assuming you have a good enough understanding of your customer's needs and wants, the rest of the book will focus on product development execution. These next steps will make sure you are able to design and build the best quality software possible, at the lowest cost possible, as quickly as possible.

Next up in Chapter Two, I'll show you how to condense the insights you glean from talking to users into an actionable plan for building your app.

---

[1] http://giffconstable.com/2012/12/12-tips-for-early-customer-development-interviews-revision-3/

CHAPTER ONE CHECKLIST

- ☐ Skim through Giff Constable's short book "Talking to Humans."
- ☐ Get out of the building and talk to at least five users.
- ☐ If you're having trouble finding users to talk to, read Jason Evanish's blog post "95 Ways to find your first customers for customer development or your first sale."
- ☐ Don't pitch your app; try to uncover your user's pain points instead.

CHAPTER TWO

WRITE USER STORIES

When most non-technical people attempt to design an app for the first time, they will often write out a laundry list of features they want. This is a recipe for failure.

The term "laundry list" originally referred to a list of clothing that had been sent to be laundered. These were basically just dumb checklists. We can do better!

Instead of defining your app as a list of features, this chapter will show you how to create a much better definition.

Define your app in terms that focus on the user's point of view; provide a "Definition of Done," or DoD, for each feature (especially handy for bug testing); and prioritize which features are most important and which you can save for later.

USER STORIES

To do this, we define our app through a list of user stories.

A user story is a one-sentence description of an interaction between a user and a product (in our case, a mobile app). User stories follow a very particular format meant to capture the connection between your product's function and the user's goal they're hiring the product to accomplish. The format conforms to this pattern:

As a (type of user), I want (some goal) so that (some reason).

Instead of collecting a laundry list of desired features from your users, user stories start with a higher purpose. Feature requests can be misleading; it's better to understand what users are trying to accomplish and then reason backward from there. What job are your customers hiring your product to do?

Once you understand your user's goals, you can begin to flesh out how your product will get them to accomplish those goals.

There are four key advantages to working with user stories:

- They communicate the user's point of view. This is crucial information for anyone you outsource to.
- They are easy to prioritize. It should be very clear to you what stories are most important and what stories are less important.
- They are easy to test/verify. When your app is built, you'll need to test it out to make sure everything works. With user stories, you can run through each story one-by-one and have full confidence that your app does what it's supposed to do.
- They leave the implementation open to interpretation. This allows your developer and designer to use their expertise to accomplish the user goal efficiently—saving you time and money.

Think about questions in this order:

- What are your users trying to accomplish?
- How does your product help them accomplish that?
- What are the steps required to accomplish it?

Each user story begins with a user persona. Developing a user persona helps you empathize with your user base. When you have thousands of users, it is impossible to represent every user. Instead, you want to group specific users together into a single profile.

Your product may have multiple types of users. For instance, Airbnb has at least two main user personas: hosts (people renting out their spaces) and travelers (people who need a place to stay).

Since your app doesn't have users yet, you're going to have to decide on a "best guess" persona based on your conversations with customers in the previous chapter. I recommend starting with no more than one or two personas; save the others for later. As Kevin Kelly, founder of WIRED magazine, says, it's better to get one thousand true fans than try to be all things to all people.[2]

To begin writing user stories, I usually pick one user persona to focus on and write as many user stories as I can think of. This is a first pass, so just write as many as you can imagine. Take a stream of consciousness approach to get everything out of your head and written down. I usually write my user stories in a spreadsheet. For an example you can copy and paste, visit appfactorysf.com/resources.

Repeat this process for the other user personas.

---

2   http://kk.org/thetechnium/1000-true-fans/

There's no hard rule about how much scope of work you can put into each story. If a story is too big, try splitting it into two stories if you can. I like to err on the side of more stories.

Once it's all out of your head, step back and sleep on it. When you wake up the next day, open the spreadsheet and force yourself to prioritize. Move the most important stories to the top and least important ones to the bottom.

Once you have a prioritized list in the spreadsheet, you need to ask yourself, "Who is the first person I will show the earliest preview of my app?" Imagine yourself showing this person a very early version of the app to get their feedback.

With that feedback in mind, take a look at your user stories and ask yourself what is the minimum number of user stories that need to be working in order to get meaningful feedback from this person? Do you really need password reset? How about updating your profile pic? Be ruthless and exclude as many as you can.

This will be hard.

By thinking in this way, you are unearthing your "minimum viable product"—a term coined by Eric Reis (one of the godfathers of the lean startup movement). The MVP contains just enough features to gather validated learning about your product and its customers.

MVP AND THE USER-ADOPTION CURVE

As a first-time non-technical founder, there are going to be lots of gaps in your design—and there should be. When building an app for the first time, you want to create an MVP, meaning it should be as basic as possible.

Even with an MVP, there are common functions many people simply forget about. A forgotten password function, a logout button, an "undo" feature if the user clicks something in error. First-time app builders often overlook all these functions.

Yes, there will be features that miss the mark the first build (maybe second and third, too), but don't worry too much about that. When launching a product for the first time, the initial batch of users is not going to be your typical app audience.

There's a user-adoption curve that I find really useful which always helps me evaluate the launch of a new product. The adoption curve shows your initial users will be very cutting-edge innovators who are willing to try out a brand new product. The masses tend to wait until an app is trending before jumping on the bandwagon.

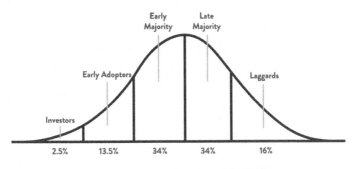

INNOVATION ADOPTION LIFECYCLE

Innovators are generally quite forgiving when there are missing pieces of the product, or if the design isn't completely refined. If you miss the mark on some things, it's okay, as long as there's a way for users to contact you so you can provide assistance and keep an open line of feedback about any missing features.

Now you'll want to visualize your MVP user stories. An easy way to do this is to copy and paste your MVP user stories from the Google spreadsheet into a Trello board—a project management tool. Here's an example:

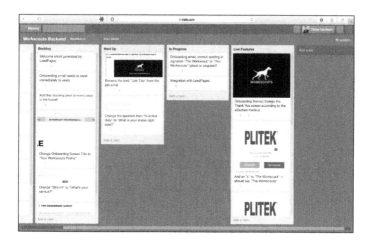

Trello provides a better visual representation of the project's progression and it allows for back-and-forth conversations on each user story. Try to maintain the prioritization of the stories by making sure the most important cards appear at the top (least important at the bottom).

Next up in Chapter Three, we're going to bring these user stories to life and begin visualizing the user interface of the app.

CHAPTER TWO CHECKLIST

☐ A user story is a one-sentence description of an interaction between a user and a product. Follow this verbal formula: "As a (type of user), I want (some goal) so that (some reason)."

☐ Write at least ten user stories into a Google Sheet. Use the template at appfactorysf.com/resources.

☐ Identify the stories that are absolutely necessary, and save the rest for later. This is your minimum viable product (MVP).

☐ Transfer the MVP stories into a Trello board. Use the template at appfactorysf.com/resources.

CHAPTER THREE

SKETCHING YOUR APP

With software, there are limits to language. Using the English language to describe software becomes tedious and ineffective. At this point, it's time to begin sketching your idea.

When I say sketch, I mean it literally. Sketch your design using good ole fashioned pen and paper. The goal is to sketch every single screen in the app, from the landing page to the sign-up page to the forgot password screen.

Sketching might seem a bit informal, but this is how all good designers start and is a helpful exercise that allows you to move beyond language and create a visual representation of your app. It's a quick and easy method that helps validate your ideas before you move on to more sophisticated and time-consuming design programs.

Using stencils of a blank device screen (iPhone, iPad, Android, web browser) can help the sketches feel more real. You can also print the stencils and simply sketch the user interface that you're imagining. To find the stencils that I use, visit appfactorysf.com/resources.

During this phase, there's no need to worry about your artistic abilities. Take it from me, I'm one of the worst artists on the planet. To prove the point, here's a portrait I drew of my wife at a dinner party some years ago.

Is that the worst portrait you've ever seen? Probably.

You don't need to be an incredible sketch artist to design your app. The point is to communicate your vision in a better, more visual way. The best designs come from repetition, reiterating on your sketches over and over until you strike gold. Continue to sketch the user interface on paper until you have a flow that you're satisfied with.

There could be an entire book (and, well, there probably is, but this isn't it) dedicated to what elements should be included in your app. I don't have all the answers here, but I do encourage you to borrow user interfaces from other apps you use and like. The UI is essentially everything you see on the screen: the collection of visual buttons and layouts that comprise an app.

You don't need to reinvent the wheel in terms of the UI for your app. Doing so would not only be a waste of time and money in the actual development phase, but the real difficulty would come post-launch. A new type of interface would be unfamiliar to your users and create a barrier to using your app. The best practice, especially in the early stages, is to borrow your user interface from other apps.

Begin by going through your favorite apps on your phone and take inspiration from what works and what doesn't work. Don't be afraid to mimic the UI of other apps, especially popular ones. The more popular the app, the more familiar the UI will be to your users—familiarity is our goal at this stage.

When sketching your UI, leave no stone unturned. Every

button in the app should flow to its eventual terminus. This means you need to know exactly what happens when you tap each button, and the next screen it leads to. Clearly understanding the flow of your screens will help limit the app features to only the essentials.

To get started, take one of your user stories and begin by sketching the necessary steps to complete the user story. Repeat this until you can run through every user story in your MVP using your sketches.

Sketching the app screens forces you to go through your own thought process and helps to ensure there's a comprehensive view of all the app requirements when you hand the project off to a developer.

When Manny, the founder of the Revive app, first came to me, he had sketches that were missing screens and had buttons representing half-baked features that were never fully brought to fruition within the context of the sketches.

I asked Manny simple questions about button functionality like, "What happens when I tap this button?" Most of the time, he didn't have an answer. If he couldn't answer those types of questions, how could a developer know what to build?

Even in some of my own work, I tend to inundate screens with features—the end result being an unrealistic app that has way too many screens. I know when I'm sketching a product and it has sixty or ninety different screens to account for, and all the buttons and features, it is a clear sign to go back to the drawing board and reprioritize.

It's difficult to pinpoint a sweet spot in regards to how many screens an app should have, but you can begin to formulate an idea by examining the navigation horizontally (how many different menu items there are to choose from), then vertically (how deep the screens go in the navigation). For the non-technical, first-time entrepreneur, 99.9 percent of the time, I would encourage them to go with fewer features. Fewer features means more manageable, cheaper, faster, and better to build.

Once you've completed your paper sketches, there are apps on the iPhone (such as Pop or Marvel, both free options) that allow you to take a photo of your sketches and add linked buttons on top of the photo. Through these apps, you can link together the sketch photos so that when you tap a button, it flows to the next screen, essentially creating a prototype that provides a pretty comprehensive view of how your app would look and feel.

Share your prototype with a friend or two and let them

click through. Ask questions about the screens and features. This simple exercise can be incredibly insightful.

You could also conduct a full-on user interview at this point, which is a more formal way to test each screen. The interview would entail asking the test user how they interpret each screen (i.e., what is the screen's function), the end result they expect from each screen, and where the screen will lead.

Beginning the interview with an objective for the test user will help flesh out the app's flow. For example, if you were building an online store where people buy sneakers, a good objective would be, "Create an account and buy a pair of sneakers."

As the user clicks on each screen, ask them these three questions on each screen:

- What are you looking at?
- What do you want to do?
- What do you expect to happen next?

The answers people give can be really surprising. A user interface that makes so much sense to you as the designer can be completely misconstrued by the average customer.

Every app is different but these sketches should be only as detailed as needed to allow the user to answer those three questions for each screen.

Sticking with the example of the e-commerce sneaker site, you might sketch out a picture of sneakers, along with the name, description, and price. As long as the test user understands the general point of the screen, you should be able to receive solid feedback.

The earlier you learn how the user interacts with your product, the better the end result will be. Creating sketches and a tappable prototype is too easy not to do. The whole process should take an hour or two, then you're in a good position to solicit feedback and go back to the literal drawing board to make any necessary tweaks to your interface.

Try the process again and see if the changes create an app that's more familiar to the user. The objective is to make your app as easy as possible to navigate and to reduce the cognitive load on the user so they are able to get what they want as soon as possible.

Keep in mind, the point of these sketches is that they should be done quickly. Sketch out what's in your head, and don't be afraid to crumple up ideas and toss them.

Once you get to later phases—beyond the sketches to the wireframes, and then into the final graphic designs—it becomes more difficult to make small tweaks to the design. Rather than a simple redrawing, tweaks might take three or four hours to make, and at that point you'll be paying a designer to make those changes.

Sketching your app to ensure all features and screens are accounted for helps you to best prepare for the later phases and will end up saving you time, money, and frustration.

CHAPTER THREE CHECKLIST

- ☐ Sketches are quick, hand-drawn mockups of the app's user interfaces.
- ☐ Sketch out ideas repeatedly and reiterate each screen until you find a flow you like.
- ☐ Apps such as Pop and Marvel turn your sketches into clickable prototypes.
- ☐ Share the prototype with others to solicit feedback.
- ☐ Return to the drawing board as many times as needed to create a user-friendly app.
- ☐ The objective is to make the app as easy as possible to navigate and to reduce the cognitive load on the user.
- ☐ The sketch phase lays the foundation for the next steps in the process.

ELEVATE YOUR SKETCHES

Sketching on paper is super-efficient. The best part is, when you mess up, you simply crumple the idea and toss it. No harm done. The sketching phase provides power and freedom to sketch the app until you're satisfied, without taking up too much of your time and money.

Once you have your pen and paper sketches complete, though, it's time to elevate them into more presentable wireframes.

Wireframes are simple black and white, low-fidelity mockups that show a developer or designer what your UI looks like. The more detailed and straightforward the wireframe, the easier it is for the people you hire to concentrate on their job, which is to elevate the wireframes to be a beautiful, high-fidelity example of what the final product will look like.

As with everything in life, balance is key. (Easier said than done, I know.) The wireframing process shouldn't exceed eight hours. Trust me, it's easy to become obsessive with details and work on the same screen for four hours straight, but it's important to continue to move forward. You always have the option of going back to screens and making adjustments if needed.

The wireframing process results in a digital wireframe file that can be used for reference and utilized when testing new features. The main objective is to help foster the feedback loop: build, measure, learn—build, measure, learn.

People use various programs to create wireframes, such as Photoshop, Justinmind, Wireframe.cc, Power MarkUp, and OmniGraffle, but all these come with a pretty steep learning curve. There are also tools like Sketch, which is less difficult to learn, but is still geared toward the more technically inclined.

I recommend a web-based tool called Balsamiq (balsamiq. com), which is perfect for non-technical people because it simplifies the wireframing process and costs only twelve dollars a month.

The first time I used Balsamiq, I needed to communicate visually what I couldn't convey with words. As we discussed, there's a point where words fail with app design, and this point often comes rather quickly.

I'd been verbally telling people about this app idea, and people would just kind of scratch their heads, clearly not understanding my vision. Once I completed the wireframes, though, my idea became much clearer to other people and the conversation totally changed.

Balsamiq provides stencils of an iPhone, along with a selection of drag and drop UI elements. If you need a back button, simply drag a back button and position it appropriately on the stenciled screen. If you need a tab bar on the bottom, drag a tab bar over and drop it into your sketch. The process is super easy and just as straightforward as it sounds.

Wireframes created with Balsamiq are clean and easy-to-read, and can be turned into an interactive prototype that can be sent through email to test users.

Having an easily shareable prototype that people can

click through is invaluable. Sharing your prototype is an important step in the app-building process, and you should be conscientious to share it with the right people.

Sending the prototype to your mom probably won't generate the critical feedback you need. Share the prototype with as many people as possible who fit your user profile. If you're developing an app for Hot Rod cars, you need feedback from Hot Rod enthusiasts. Makes sense, right?

Soliciting feedback from and interacting with your target audience during the wireframing phase will help prepare you to make more informed decisions regarding the end product.

MORE IS BETTER

Creating wireframes is an art that requires a deliberate balance, but I personally tend to include as much detail as possible. The prototype should be as real as possible in order to accurately test the UI and screen flow. When you share the prototype with someone for testing, you want their minds to be free of bias and the experience to feel real.

Let's look at how I would create a wireframe for a user profile. First, I include all the standard content, like the name of the user, a real profile photo, and a description. If you use filler text that doesn't really make sense, like the letters ABCDEFG in the name field, the people testing your app will be caught off guard and their brain is going to get stuck on the bit of information that's out of place. Your goal is to get feedback on the core of the product, not little details that maybe you were too hasty to include, such as filling out realistic dummy data.

Producing a realistic prototype not only provides a more true-to-life test user experience, it ultimately helps to strengthen the overall product. In the case of selling sneakers through an e-commerce store, each pair of sneakers needs a name, product description, price, etc.

Including the nitty-gritty information into the wireframes will also enforce the space constraints on the screen. Product descriptions, for example, have character limits, but this constraint is often overlooked until the development phase.

Determining constraints and limits on your own time (and dime) will save money in the long run. Rather than the developer or designer you hire being the one to tell you the descriptions are too long, and going back and forth, entering all the seemingly superfluous information into the wireframes helps flesh out the appropriate constraints in advance.

OPTIONAL STEP: TO HIRE A GRAPHIC DESIGNER OR NOT?

How beautiful does your app need to be? How beautiful does your MVP need to be? Graphic designers are great—and they can make your app beautiful and delightful—but not every MVP needs to be beautiful. Remember, your MVP needs to be nimble and adaptable. Locking into a specific design may hurt more than it helps.

Most software developers aren't good visual artists. They tend to be left-brain oriented, specializing in logical analysis. To create beautiful graphics for your app, you need a right-brain oriented creative specialist. Enter the graphic designer.

There are benefits to hiring a graphic designer. Beautiful graphics can really improve the user experience of the MVP and also increase the trust users place in your product. All of this costs more time and money, of course. As the entrepreneur, you'll need to make the final judgment on this cost-benefit analysis.

Another thing to be aware of: sometimes designers get a little "too excited" and want to add features that will cost you more money to build. Make sure they're staying within the bounds of the MVP scope.

Expect to pay $500–$4,000 for a graphic designer to take your wireframes and turn them into designs.

The good news is the wireframes you already created will be a godsend to a graphic designer. You've already created the canvas, now they just need to paint the colors.

The wireframes become extremely relevant and useful in the graphic design phase. Having neat and organized wireframes gives the designer a better understanding of your vision. The better the designer understands your vision, the more creativity you're allowing them.

If you would like to hire a graphic designer, check out the Appendix section titled "Hiring a Graphic Designer" for step-by-step instructions at the end of this book.

CHAPTER FOUR CHECKLIST

☐ Balsamiq is a web-based tool that really simplifies the wireframing process for non-technical people.

☐ Include all the nitty-gritty information in the wireframes.

☐ Balsamiq creates an easy-to-read prototype file that can be emailed to test users for feedback.

☐ Wireframes will help in the graphic design phase.

☐ Wireframes help to tighten the feedback loop by eliminating the need to go all the way back to the sketching phase.

CHAPTER FIVE

CREATE THE PRODUCT SPEC

The product spec is basically the Holy Grail of your project.

Creating the product spec is the responsibility of you, the entrepreneur, and should be based on your product vision. This is the document you will provide to potential developers during the interview process so they can provide an accurate timeline and quote, and suggest the best tools for the project.

The product spec defines every screen from the wireframe, the app functions and features, and all the project requirements. The ultimate goal is to convey to the freelance team what the finished product should look like and how it should function. With that in mind, the document should read like easy-to-follow instructions for all freelancers working on your project, especially the developer and graphic designer.

The tool I find best for building your product spec is Google Slides. Similar to PowerPoint, Google Slides makes it really easy to control screens, share them with others, and allow for in-line comments and feedback.

The product spec starts with a product overview, describing the mission of the product, the target user, and the operating system supported. For example, iOS versions and iPhone models: Apple Support[3] offers up-to-date statistics on the percentage of users using each iOS. This will help you determine which system(s) you should focus

---

3   https://developer.apple.com/support/app-store/

on. The overview should also include a link to the interactive wireframes on Balsamiq, so your freelance team can instantly pull up that clickable prototype.

Next, provide a high-level functional requirement overview describing all the features within the app. The list could include features such as a notification center, sign up with Facebook capability, or the ability to pay for goods.

Each feature should then be broken down further into bulleted lists, detailing the specific requirements for each. In the instance of the notification function, list the types of notifications, the push notifications that you want to support, when a user will receive a notification, etc. Include more concrete examples of how to break down features and their functions.

Every screen within the app has its own slide that explains exactly what the screen is and how it functions. The screen explanations are the bulk of the product spec. Each one of these slides displays a screenshot on the left side, and then on the right has a description of what is on the screen. Include a screenshot of your example.

If I were creating a screen explanation slide for the user sign-up page, I would insert the screenshot and detail the type of sign-ups the app will accept. For example, people can sign up with email or through Facebook. When they sign up with email, we're going to send them a confirmation email to verify their email address. And when they sign up with Facebook, we're going to collect their name, their birthday, and their email address.

The objective is to describe as many elements on the screen as possible by explaining what they are and the next steps when a user interacts with them. When a user taps the sign up with Facebook button, what happens next? Walking through the functionality and flow creates a detailed map, which will help the developer understand the screens they need to build and the requirements of each.

BENEFITS OF THE PRODUCT SPEC

Sketching and wireframing are steps that help you to better understand the app, so you have more accurate and thoughtful information to create the product spec. The first two steps feed into the last, but they all ultimately help to better communicate your vision to the developer and designer.

Communication is the best way to ensure the final product accurately mirrors your vision. If you approach your freelance team with a vague idea like, "I want to build an app where you can connect with people in your area," odds are the product they create won't align with your vision...at all.

Taking the necessary steps to ensure the final product will meet your expectations not only saves you a ton of time and money, it makes the jobs of your freelance team easier. Good developers and designers want to create a product that exceeds your standards; so, by providing specific instructions and requirements, you're helping to eliminate a lot of the guesswork and anxiety from their perspective.

The other benefit of creating a product spec is that it continues the process of helping you think through your product. When you are forced to define every screen and specify exactly what needs to happen, you evaluate your product in a very detailed way.

Through this process, you're likely to find gaps in the functionality you previously overlooked or functionality that is overly tedious. Again, these steps allow you to adjust your vision before getting to the development and design phase where, as we know, time is money.

ANDROID VS. IPHONE & SUBMITTING YOUR APP

A question that often comes up for first-time non-technical

founders is the need to support multiple devices (i.e., Android, iPhone, etc.). The answer relies heavily on the target user of the app.

What devices are potential customers using? Examining the needs and preferences of your customers in the wireframe phase should have provided insight into their preferred device(s).

In general, all things made equal, I typically target iOS first and there are a few reasons for that. The main reason being that statistically, Android users spend substantially less money than iPhone users, meaning iOS customers are more inclined to make purchases and spend money within an app. As recently as 2014, Apple users are spending four times more than Google users.

From a more technical standpoint, Android has notorious fragmentation problems because there are so many different Android devices that come in various shapes and sizes and operate on many different types of operating systems.

Unlike Apple, Google doesn't have one universal operating system with different versions. On top of that, Android devices often have different types of operating system implementations depending on carrier.

Various device sizes and types, along with a multitude of different operating systems, quickly translate to tens of thousands of different combinations, which can create a highly fragmented product.

The fragmentation makes it difficult for the app developer to conduct proper bug testing, and is ultimately why Android apps are notoriously buggy. Big app companies have large teams dedicated to testing an app on hundreds of devices, and even they can't test them all. A first-time entrepreneur won't have the time, resources, or money to accomplish this scale of testing.

Again, all things being equal, the only reason to launch your app with Android first would be if it requires a function that Apple doesn't allow. Android has a more open system and cedes a lot of the control to the app founders. Apple, on the other hand, has a much more closed system and they restrict access to certain phone features (like the homescreen, for example).

Another downside of iOS is the review time. Every time you submit a version of the app, it takes up to two weeks to be approved or declined, pending review from their app board. With Android, app approval is generally instant.

Apple Support does offer a set of documents, called the

Apple App Store Review Guidelines, that's worth a read through before entering the development phase. There are all sorts of reasons why Apple's decline rate is higher.

For instance, Apple is very strict on the way Apple Pay is integrated into iOS apps. Any app that uses Apple Pay needs to use the branded Apple Pay button and display the full transaction receipt before purchase. If you're using Apple Pay, you can't create a generic "Pay Now" button and provide your own transaction record.

I've had apps declined by Apple for not being 100 percent faithful to their guidelines. I once had an app declined for featuring the word "Beta" on its logo. The review guidelines don't allow the word beta anywhere in an app because Apple only wants finished products in the app store.

But, I'll let you in on a little trick I've learned: If you can find another app on the app store that violates the same rule, but has somehow slid under the review board's radar, then nine times out of ten the board will reverse its decision to decline your app.

The approval process can be scary at times because you never know what the review board will say, but reading through the guidelines should help to deter from any unnecessary setbacks.

A solid piece of advice, though: Don't plan your launch date until you've been approved by the app store. I've seen many founders plan big launch parties two weeks after they submit to the app store, only to be declined, which leads to an embarrassing situation.

CHAPTER FIVE CHECKLIST

☐ The product spec defines every screen, the app functions and features, and all the project requirements.

☐ Google Slides is the best tool for creating a product spec.

☐ The product spec should read as an instructional guide for the developer.

☐ The goal of any first-time app creator is to create a minimum viable product.

☐ The initial users of an app are cutting-edge innovators, not your typical app purchaser.

☐ Apps for iOS are significantly easier to build, integrate, and bug test.

☐ Android has a more open system and cedes a lot of the control to the app founders.

HIRE A ROCK STAR FREELANCE DEVELOPER

The single biggest pitfall for non-technical entrepreneurs is hiring the wrong developer.

I like to think of the developer as the digital carpenter. I picture them wearing a hardhat, hacking away at their keyboard, taking the ideas from the wireframes and product spec and turning them into code.

Like a carpenter building a house, developers build the necessary technical infrastructure to support and launch an app. There's a lot of work that you don't see—like plumbing hidden in the walls. We call that part of the app the "back end," while the "front end" is everything the user can see when they use the app.

The back end is basically a computer stored in the Cloud that houses the app database, serving data back and forth between the app on a phone and the database in the Cloud. Yes, this is the part where things get technical and slightly confusing.

Software requires a computer to run on, but if an app relies solely on the handheld device's computer, app performance won't be optimized. To increase app optimization and centralize the database, a lot of heavy computing tasks are outsourced to a computer that lives in the so-called Cloud. The job of the developer extends beyond what you see on the screen, as there's a whole lot of behind-the-scenes infrastructure required to support an app.

All the steps you've taken up until this point—writing user stories, wireframing, creating a product spec—will be hugely valuable during the developer hiring process. Because you've taken the time to fully define the product, you can more accurately communicate what you want and refine your search, pre-emptively weeding out candidates who don't have the expertise or skill for your project.

This kind of vetting is extremely difficult and time-consuming for non-technical founders. Properly judging the talent and knowledge of developers requires an extremely specific set of technical skills. Developers speak their own language, which makes it next to impossible for a non-technical person to be able to gauge their skills.

As a non-technical entrepreneur, you need a way to quickly find developers who are expert level in the languages and frameworks your app requires. The first challenge: figuring out what languages and frameworks your app requires. The second challenge: finding a developer who is expert level at those specific things.

These are challenges I struggled with for three years. Over that time, I experimented with lots of different approaches: recruiting through Craigslist, hiring on freelance marketplaces like Upwork, reaching out directly via LinkedIn. But there's one solution that delivered results ten times above all others, and that I still use to this day.

The solution? Toptal.

The revolutionary concept behind Toptal is to connect entrepreneurs with the best, most elite level of professional freelancers. Toptal conducts all the necessary technical interviews and handles the hours and hours of test projects and code reviews necessary to ensure every developer on their roster is not just good—they're really, really good.

Not only does Toptal take time and effort to vet the most talented freelancers, they're equally as diligent at screening potential clients in order to ensure every project they accept will be a good fit for their developers as well. It's not like Craigslist, where anyone can create an ad and find a developer.

Toptal is selective about who uses their platform because, in order to maintain their elite roster of freelance talent, they need to provide their freelancers with valuable work and protect them against bad project managers. This means Toptal will thoroughly vet you as a founder prior to granting you access to their platform.

All the preparation steps I've prescribed up until this point (the product spec, wireframes, value prop canvas, and sketches), are intended to help improve your chances of working with Toptal. Approaching Toptal with a vague, half-baked idea—hey, I have this idea, it's like Facebook... but for hip hop fans!—will result in a thanks, but no thanks.

You must present them with a detailed plan, mapped out screens, defined features, and basic designs. These elements prove your vision is fully formed and that you're serious about creating a viable, valuable product. With these assets established, Toptal will be much more likely to take on your project and help you find a super-talented developer.

Having worked with Toptal in the past, I have an account manager, through whom I make client referrals. Through the referral process, the client receives a $1,000 rebate on their project if they choose to move forward with a Toptal developer. If you'd like to go through Toptal, which is my strong recommendation, here are the next steps.

BEFORE TOPTAL

Prior to bringing your project to Toptal, you might want to consider hiring a consultant to help ensure you have all the necessary details needed to move forward. The app-building process involves many micro-decisions that, as a first-time founder, you might not be aware of.

WHICH PLATFORM IS BEST FOR YOUR NEEDS?

Determining which platform will best help achieve your goals is likely an area in which you'll need outside help. Utilizing a consultant who can sort through wireframes and bring their insight to determine the best approach from a technology perspective can help you choose the right platform, which will establish the type of developer you should be looking to hire.

NATIVE OR WEB?

There's a classic debate in the tech world between web apps and native apps. There's no clear answer, but it's an important decision to make.

When building a mobile app, there are two basic ways to go about it. One is to build what's called a native app, which is how most of the apps on the app store are built. A native app has the software natively running on the device.

A web app, or hybrid app, basically has a native wrapper around a website. You may have noticed some apps are a bit slower to respond and don't have the same type of animations. These apps feel different because they're actually websites that are designed to appear as apps.

The native approach costs more money but provides a much cleaner and more stable experience. Users can stay logged in and access more device features, like the camera or location services. A web app is typically cheaper to develop, and developers are able to update the app in the background, without having to submit to Apple.

For early-stage startups, I tend to err on the side of web apps because this approach allows for product changes to be made quickly. In the early stages, the two-week review period that's enforced any time you implement changes to a native app can be detrimental.

That being said, there's no right answer across the board, and the best type of app for you will depend on a lot of factors.

TOPTAL INTRODUCTION

The next step is to email me (drew@appfactorysf.com) with your project details. If needed, we can set up a Skype call to further discuss the scope and goals of your project, or I can forward you directly to my account manager at Toptal. Through my introduction, you'll be eligible for that $1,000 rebate if you end up hiring one of their developers.

After I introduce you to the Toptal account manager, they will set up a phone call to discuss the project and its requirements. Their goal is to get a sense of your expectations and budget to help determine whether they can help you.

This is the point where the Toptal team interviews you to ensure your project is sane and well-defined. If you ask them to build YouTube in two weeks, for example, they're going to flag that as an unrealistic expectation and will likely conclude they aren't the best fit for your project.

USING TOPTAL

If Toptal chooses to move forward with your project, the next step is to create an account. Their account management system sets up your job, which is a detailed description of your project. Once your job is established in the system, Toptal begins searching for developers in their network who meet your needs.

Toptal works diligently to find developers who have experience in the features that you will be implementing. If you're using Stripe for payments, they'll search for someone who has experience with Stripe. If you're looking for an iOS front-end developer, they'll find a couple of candidates who match that description. Their goal is to match you with potential developers who have a solid history of projects with overlapping skillsets.

Once they've matched your project with a couple of prospects, they send you the candidates. Typically, they match you with three or four candidates over the period of a week and instruct you to set up Skype interviews with each of them.

The advantage here is that there's no need to go into the technical nitty-gritty because Toptal has already conducted the technical interviews with all their developers. Everyone they recommend is vetted, but there are certain points you want to make sure to hit during the developer interviews.

INTERVIEW CHECKLIST

- ☐ Have they read the product spec?
- ☐ Is their time estimate in line with your budget?
- ☐ Does their past experience overlap with the skills you need?
- ☐ Do they understand the product and vision?
- ☐ How do they communicate?
- ☐ Are they open to daily stand-up meetings?
- ☐ Do they charge a weekly rate?

Now, let's go through each item on the checklist.

HAVE THEY READ THE PRODUCT SPEC?

First and foremost, you want to make sure they've read the product spec prior to the interview. If they haven't, that's a bad sign and you should cross them off your list of potential candidates.

IS THEIR TIME ESTIMATE IN LINE WITH YOUR BUDGET?

If they're properly prepared, they should be able to provide a rough timeline and recommend any resources or third-party software that could speed up the development process.

A helpful side note when it comes to time estimates: if a developer says a project will take them four weeks, plan for six to eight weeks. Developers tend to underestimate timelines, so my general rule of thumb is to adjust the project expectations to one-and-a-half to two times their estimate.

Skewed timelines are a classic development problem that most likely stem from the fact that developers are proud of their skills, but the reality is that the project will typically take longer than the initial projections.

DOES THEIR PAST EXPERIENCE OVERLAP WITH THE SKILLS YOU NEED?

Ask candidates about past projects, their approach to new jobs, and, most importantly, how these two factors make them a good fit for your project.

DO THEY UNDERSTAND THE PRODUCT AND VISION?

Their answers will demonstrate how closely related their

experience is to your project and allow you to glean how well they understand your product and overall vision.

HOW DOES THE DEVELOPER COMMUNICATE?

Perhaps one of the more important points to flesh out during interviews is whether the developer seems to be communicative. Communication is vital to success when working with a remote freelancer, and you must ascertain whether you could trust this person to maintain an open dialogue throughout the development process. There are plenty of rock star developers out there who aren't effective because they don't have the ability to communicate well.

ARE THEY OPEN TO DAILY STAND-UP MEETINGS?

Communication means proactively sending updates and being open to daily stand-up meetings. If a developer is against participating in daily stand-up meetings, they're not the right fit for a first-time founder. In order to create the best product possible, stay true to your vision and learn along the way. You need to keep your fingers on the pulse of the project, which is the reason for the daily stand-ups. We will cover stand-up meetings in depth in the next chapter.

DO THEY CHARGE A WEEKLY RATE?

Developers that work through Toptal typically charge a weekly rate, which guarantees your bills will remain consistent and you won't ever be surprised with an unusually exorbitant bill.

Weekly rates for each developer Toptal suggests are accessible during the interview process so you're able to compare prices before hiring.

An important note: rates are relatively irrespective of skill and are generally more dependent on the freelancer's geographic location and cost of living.

Again, this is an odd phenomenon when hiring from the global talent pool that seems counterintuitive to your knowledge as a businessperson; but, in many cases, someone from overseas who charges $1,200 per week is likely just as skilled as someone from the United States who charges $3,000 per week. The developers are simply in two drastically different economic environments, which accounts for the disparity between prices.

Rates also fluctuate depending on the type of developer you're hiring. It's true, not all developers are created equal. A Ruby on Rails developer might cost about $1,400–$1,500 per week, where an iOS developer costs more in the range of $1,800–$2,000 per week.

Certain languages are in high demand and have developers in short supply (iOS, Android), while other languages have a more abundant supply of developers, which lowers the cost associated with them. Mastering Ruby on Rails, for example, takes significantly less time and effort than iOS, so developers with this skillset are more abundant, effectively driving down the cost.

Interview at least three to four candidates before you make any hiring decisions. Especially because this will be your first time in the project management position, it's important to compare candidates and accurately gauge your expectations versus your options.

Another mistake first-time non-technical entrepreneurs tend to make is hiring more than one developer for their project. Sure, it sounds like a good idea in theory; the more developers, the quicker the project is completed, right? But managing multiple developers on one project is much more work than it seems.

For your first project, stick with one developer.

ONE-WEEK TRIAL PERIOD

Another revolutionary and helpful feature Toptal offers is a one-week, risk-free trial period with every developer you hire. This allows you to work with a developer for a full week to gauge the effectiveness of their communication and whether they will be able to deliver results within the projected timeline.

The one-week trial period allows you to effectively "fire" the developer if they aren't meeting your standards. If you do choose to end your working relationship with the developer during the trial period, you will not be charged and Toptal immediately begins searching for new candidates. You're allowed as many one-week trial periods as you need in order to find someone who you can successfully work with.

THE LOGISTICS

Once you secure your developer, you'll work with a sales engineer who acts as a coordinator between you and the freelancer. The freelancer tracks their time (if paid by the hour) and reports it to the sales engineer who maintains the billing information and posts bills to your account on a weekly basis.

From the time the bill posts, you have a week or two to

settle up. Toptal accepts credit cards, but you get a 3 percent discount by connecting your bank account and paying through a bank transfer.

OTHER OPTIONS

There are other freelance websites out there. One example is a company called Gigster, which also has a global pool of developers. Their model is a hybrid between agency and software as a service, and their market differentiator is that they provide project quotes within fifteen minutes.

It's an interesting concept, but the issue is you're back to the black box agency model where you have no involvement in the development process. As I noted previously, cutting yourself out of the loop as a non-technical co-founder prevents you from learning about the product development experience or process, and you're not asserting your value as an entrepreneur.

There are also freelance marketplaces, like Upwork, where founders can post jobs and freelance professionals are able to bid on work. Broadly, I've heard mixed reviews about Upwork, the biggest problem being that it's built for technical people who know what to look for.

Despite Upwork's marketing that appeals to the

non-technical audience, the issue remains that, as a non-technical person, you're in charge of conducting technical interviews with prospective developers. Again, deep technical knowledge is needed to test developers and rigorously review their work.

Unfortunately, if I examine the experiences of non-technical entrepreneurs who've used Upwork to hire a developer, almost every person I've spoken with shares a similar horror story that resulted in lost time, money, and motivation. The issue, again, being that people with a non-technical background simply don't have the expertise needed to vet and hire the best developer for the project.

Most of these stories are of people who pay what seems like a bargain rate for a developer, only to have the time-line extended again and again. And, in the end, they're presented with either nothing or an app far different from their vision.

Upwork does have a dispute resolution process, but from what I've heard this only works when you receive a fixed project price. Many contractors will attempt to move you to an hourly rate; that way you have to pay for their time spent on the project. Unfortunately, Upwork and other marketplaces can be infiltrated with scammers, and, when you're not well-versed in the industry, it's difficult to pinpoint them in advance.

Not to say there aren't a lot of really great developers on the Upwork platform; the problem is finding those people. In order to find them, you have to be technically inclined. Working with Toptal initially is kind of like having training wheels that help navigate you through the development process.

Hopefully, after a few projects with Toptal, you'll learn more about the hiring process, what to look for in developers, and how to approach the needs of your project. Once you've established yourself as an authoritative project manager and become a true outsourcing master, you can experiment with platforms like Upwork.

CHAPTER SIX CHECKLIST

- ☐ The single biggest pitfall for newbie non-technical product managers is hiring the wrong developer.
- ☐ Developer rates are relatively irrespective of skill and are generally more dependent on the freelancer's geographic location and cost of living.
- ☐ For your first project, work with only one developer; managing multiple developers on one project is much more work than it seems.

- ☐ Toptal conducts all the necessary technical interviews and code reviews and hires the top 3 percent of freelancers who apply to be on their platform.
- ☐ The client is also screened by Toptal to ensure their elite developers are offered only well-planned, fully formed project ideas.
- ☐ Toptal offers a one-week trial period.
- ☐ Other marketplace options exacerbate the issues for non-technical founders.

CHAPTER SEVEN

MANAGING THE PROJECT

As project manager, your job is to empower the developer and ensure they're firing on all cylinders in order to maintain their timeline throughout the project.

There are many points in the process where developers can get stuck. The project manager is responsible for troubleshooting those problem areas so the developer can move forward at full speed.

The product spec does a lot of the heavy lifting of communicating the requirements and features to the developer. As questions arise, the developer should be able to refer to the product spec for answers, which saves a lot of hassle and allows the process to quickly move along.

Whether working with an agency or a freelancer, lack of communication about the project can result in debilitating issues that, sadly, don't become apparent to the founder until the end of the process.

To keep the communication frequent, I recommend all project managers have daily stand-up meetings with their developer. This is a daily opportunity to discuss what was accomplished, the plan for the next day, and whether the developer experienced any blockers in their work.

A stand-up meeting is really short, just five minutes or so, and allows you to keep your finger on the pulse of the project. You can ask your developer questions like, "What did you work on today? What are you going to work on tomorrow? Are there any blockers in your way?" Just by having this daily check-in, you're building a relationship with your developer and are able to verify that they're making progress.

If your developer has blockers in their way, your job is to help eliminate them so the project can continue progressing. One of the advantages of working with people offshore, in say, Eastern Europe, China, or India, is you're able to develop a fast-moving twenty-four-hour work loop.

Your morning is the end of their workday, so you can take any blockers or issues that come up in the daily stand-ups and work on them throughout the day. While your developer is sleeping, you can produce the resources they need and they can move forward come the beginning of their workday.

Another helpful communication tool is Slack, which is a more efficient alternative to email. Slack is a free chat program that provides real-time messaging and file sharing capabilities. Having all communications stored in one conversation channel provides a project database, helps eliminate misunderstandings, and allows for quicker response times.

BLOCKERS

Many times, blockers are easy fixes, such as creating the necessary user accounts or supplying graphic assets. The developer might come across a missing element, such as a screen, that they want to suggest adding in. Or, your developer might be setting up the payment portal, but first you need to create an account on Stripe.

Despite your best efforts, it's impossible to think of everything before kicking off a project. Inevitably, you'll run into issues and need to make decisions on things you hadn't thought of before. You must be responsive and able to address issues and concerns throughout the process.

DEMOS

Schedule one to two demos throughout the week in addition to the daily stand-up meetings. Demos can take place at the same time as your daily stand-up, but are longer meetings that generally take up to a half hour. Demos are more one-on-one, and the developer can screen share over Google Hangouts or Skype to show you the app and the progress they've made.

The approach to take with developers is simple: trust but verify. If they tell you they're working on X feature and Y feature, trust them, but then verify that both X and Y features are complete during the demos.

MANAGING EXPECTATIONS

Through Toptal, you're generally hiring a full-time developer, which means your project should be their only focus and they should be putting in forty hours per week of work.

During the initial developer meeting, there are a few points you definitely want to cover, including running through the product spec together and breaking the project down into smaller milestones.

Once the project is broken into milestones, ask the developer to assign deadlines to each milestone. Deadlines aren't really set in stone, but getting the developer to commit to a timeline on the first meeting sets expectations from the very beginning. If you want to get granular, you can also develop daily milestones, such as complete the sign-in flow, develop purchase flow, and integrate payment system.

Defining clear expectations will help you, as a project manager, monitor the progress and overall project health throughout the development process. Without the milestone markers, it's difficult to gauge the project's progress.

If the developer misses one or two deadlines, there's usually an issue with the timeline, not necessarily their work. However, if they start missing several deadlines, then that's a red flag something might not be right.

If the timeline is deviated from, the best approach is to immediately discuss the issue and try to identify the cause. If you can understand why a deadline is missed, you can determine whether there's a legitimate reason.

In most cases, there are legitimate reasons why a deadline

gets pushed back, and understanding those reasons will help you judge how to move forward. Maybe Facebook changed its API or iOS updated to a new version that totally messed up a feature. Hiccups happen and you might need to alter your process to help the developer better achieve deadlines.

A lot of the time, deadlines are pushed back because the app founder doesn't have all the necessary resources in place before beginning development. Cases where the project manager fails to prepare are hugely frustrating for developers because it forces them to sit in limbo while the founder troubleshoots. Developers like to move fast, not wait around for you to figure out the next steps. The preparation I've prescribed helps to ensure you won't run into any hugely detrimental issues in the development process.

Of course, there will be instances when a developer doesn't deliver what they promised, and this boils down to your own judgment of character. As the project manager, you have to determine whether they are meeting expectations.

Having the daily stand-ups and check-ins should help you maintain a good read on the situation. Typically, when deadlines and timelines begin to be problematic, it's because the entrepreneur is not an active participant in the process.

GETTING THE JOB DONE WITH THE RIGHT TOOLS

Using the right tools will greatly enhance your efficiency and effectiveness as a product manager. Luckily, thanks to that same technological revolution that's made it possible for you to build an app in the first place, there's an arsenal of tools readily available that can help you along the way.

THE COMMUNICATION STACK

Together, these tools comprise what I call the communications stack: Google Hangouts or Skype for daily stand-up meetings and Slack for any kind of additional project. For milestone tracking, I recommend a website called Trello, which is a funnel-based project management tool that allows you to track project milestones and deadlines.

PROJECT MANAGEMENT

Trello provides a comprehensive way to manage project details, such as what's in production, what's being worked on currently (this week), and what's in the immediate and more distant future. You can create different boards for each phase of product development and add cards for each milestone to its corresponding board.

At a glance, you can see exactly what features are live,

what features are being worked on, and what features are in the backlog.

FILE SHARING

For basic file sharing and storage, Dropbox is a good tool to use because you can quickly and efficiently share big graphics files.

CODE HOSTING

GitHub allows for more collaborative software development and focuses on what they call version control. Developers can "commit their code" to Github on a daily basis, which basically means they save that version of code. This serves as a backup for their code in case their computer crashes, and it also provides access to earlier versions of the code.

Say I was working on a project and somehow the code that I wrote today broke the app and, for lack of a better term, screwed everything up. With Github, there's no need to panic because I can go back to yesterday's saved code base and start again from there, with the new knowledge to not repeat the same mistake.

As the non-technical founder, you create the Github

account for the developer to use, but you personally won't have much interaction with the platform. The main reason you'd interact with Github is to verify the developer is working throughout the project and making regular commits.

GitHub does offer a free version, but then your code is visible to everyone in the world, so I recommend upgrading to the micro plan, which is only seven dollars per month and makes your repositories private so only you can see them.

CHAPTER SEVEN CHECKLIST

- ☐ Daily stand-up meetings are imperative to maintaining control and tracking progress.
- ☐ The initial developer meeting should establish milestones and timelines to accurately gauge project progression.
- ☐ The project manager is responsible for fixing blockers so the developer can continue their work.
- ☐ There's typically a reason for deadlines being missed; don't overreact until the details are known.
- ☐ Demos help ensure the developer transparency.
- ☐ Utilize project management tools to create a more efficient, streamlined process.

PROVIDING FEEDBACK

A project going completely as expected is rare, but problems don't typically arise until the end of development when you get into the bug-testing phase.

Imagine you are building water pipes in five different cities and need them all to connect in one place. In the building phase, each city has its own pipe system that, standing alone, seems to function great.

As the project progresses, the pipes get closer and closer to the site where they're going to connect. Keeping track of all the separate pipelines is relatively simple, but the chaotic part comes at the very end when it's time to join them together. At this point, you could find out one of the angles of the pipes from city C is off by two degrees, causing the pipes to end up a couple hundred yards away from where they need to be.

In essence, this is bug testing.

Software development can experience similar issues. You have many complex pieces that you're building in silos, and you have to stitch them all together at the end. Until this point, you can't accurately know how much time and work is remaining in the project.

Bug testing is typically the most frustrating part of the process because it's the phase non-technical people are least prepared for psychologically. To be blunt, it can be a really scary process for non-technical and technical founders alike. Your product is your baby. This app is the thing you've been dreaming of for months and, in your mind, you imagine a perfect, beautiful end product.

However, the reality of the process is, the only way to get to that perfect, beautiful app is through bug testing. When entering the bug-testing phase, it's important to realize one undeniable fact: there's no such thing as a bug-free app.

The reality is all apps have bugs, and yours won't be the exception. Even Facebook's app still has bugs! My

Facebook app crashes all the time and they have a team of probably over one hundred people continuously testing the app, and even more people working on it from the technical side.

Your gut reaction during the bug-testing phase might veer toward frustration and disappointment because the buggy app you're working with is far from the perfect finished product you'd imagined. At this point, just remember: Facebook, one of the most popular, widespread, viral apps out there still has bugs. Allow that to resonate for a second, take a deep breath, and move on.

Once you accept there will be bugs in your app, you can fully understand that the bug-testing phase will not only improve your app, but that you, as the founder and project manager, will play an active role in this improvement process.

Software is a constantly evolving, constantly improving enterprise.

This is the stage where you, as the non-technical founder, can really make a difference and take action to improve your app. This should be an exciting time because you can get your hands dirty and dig into the process.

Some first-time non-technical founders assume bug

testing is the responsibility of the developer. Essentially, all development is bug testing. A developer's job is to type out codes, see if they work, and then fix them if necessary. At the end of the day, the developer's bug testing isn't sufficient.

Think of writers, who stare at the same words on the screen for hours and hours a day. Eventually, it becomes difficult for them to see the errors and typos in their own work, which is why writers have editors. The same is true for software development.

Developers are entrenched in the same code for hours on end, which inevitably causes the same blindness to errors that writers experience. They need a second set of eyes to go over their work, and that's where you, the non-technical founder, come into play.

Another important note: Developers hate bugs just as much as you do, if not more. Perhaps one of the most frustrating parts of being a developer is bug testing, because finding the bug is like searching for the needle in a haystack.

A developer might spend hours combing through the code, trying to find where the error is and at the end of their search, discover there's a missing semicolon in the code. Plug that semicolon in and everything is functioning smoothly again. Imagine that.

The process is painful. Imagine reading over the same code twenty times and not seeing that missing semicolon, but then finally it clicks.

When you encounter a bug, report it to your developer in the most descriptive way possible to help pinpoint where the issue might be. Being specific and detailed will aid the developer and help guarantee the bugs are fixed as quickly as possible. In the end, efficiency saves time and money, and you help to improve the overall app quality.

I've worked with many clients who approach bug testing the wrong way. The founder simply reports that the home screen isn't working. From the developer's standpoint, this tells them almost nothing about the bug, how to find it, or, most importantly, how to fix it.

The developer needs more information:

- What is the home screen supposed to be doing that it's not doing?
- What happens when you uninstall and reinstall the app?
- What device and operating system are you using?
- Do you have screenshots or video?

Being as specific and descriptive as possible, you should reproduce the steps leading up to the bug because these are critical for the developer to understand. If the developer can't reproduce the issue you're experiencing, there's no way for them to fix the problem.

So, when approaching bugs, describe the exact problem: When I hit the refresh button on the home screen, the app gets stuck loading and never refreshes. When I force quit and reopen, the app reverts back to normal, but the refreshing problem still persists when I try again. I'm using an iPhone 7, running iOS 10.3.1, and here are some screenshots of what I'm seeing on my device.

Detailed information will help the developer pinpoint the issue, which could be a myriad of things. The bug could manifest on the iPhone 6, but not the iPhone 5, for instance, so that information is crucial to helping them find the bug.

The most traditional approach to bug testing is to wait until the app is feature complete before beginning, but I recommend bug testing often, as soon as you have an early build. The app won't be feature complete yet, and might have some missing screens, but it should be enough to test the milestones you identified alongside your developer.

Testing early allows you to be proactive and helps stop bugs from spreading. A bug in one part of the app could very possibly mess up another part of the app, so testing as you build is kind of like clipping weeds early, before they become too big.

Of course, if you'd prefer to wait until the end to bug test, that's fine, assuming your project is relatively well-scoped. A four-week project build is a manageable timeframe, but a six-month project timeline is too long to wait to begin testing. Continuously bug testing would be much more manageable and efficient.

"Delivering a build" should be one of the milestones mapped out during the initial kickoff meeting with your developer. For example, midway through the project, the developer should deliver a build that has features X, Y, and Z, in order to bug test those components.

Big organizations typically have an entire quality assurance (QA) department dedicated to bug testing. The QA department and the development department are set up as adversaries within the company. The developers are constantly shipping new code to the QA people, who are constantly sending it back saying, no, this doesn't work, this doesn't work, this doesn't work. There's generally a bit of friendly competition—the QA people find as many bugs as they can, and the developers kill as many bugs as they can.

In your case, you are the QA department and your job is extremely important.

Of course, nothing is ever perfect. (Are you sensing a pattern here?) Even post-launch, you will encounter bugs in your app; but that's okay because, despite your grandiose vision of launching the perfect app, one of the main launch goals is to get more bug testers.

With this in mind, a word to the wise: don't blow the entire project budget on the first build. There will be bugs, upgrades, and other changes you will have to implement after the app is released.

Retaining your developer on an hourly basis during the launch will help ensure they're available to troubleshoot and fix issues as needed.

To ensure you're able to fix as many bugs as possible, you'll want to have a support system in the app. A help button that launches an email dialogue that is sent to support@ yourapp.com, for example. This allows people to notify you when they experience an issue, at which point you can obtain as many details as possible about the issue, the device being affected, the operating system, etc.

Crash analytic software, like Crashlytics, is a helpful tool that automatically reports to you every time the app crashes. The report includes error log details that the developer can use to track down the issue and reproduce the bug.

Early on, direct communication with your users is advisable. When you launch an app for the first time, you're probably only going to have a handful of users. Maintaining close communication with these early adapters is a great way to learn about how they're using the app and any issues they're experiencing.

Once issues begin to arise, you'll want to prioritize them and tackle the highest priority ones first. This is another point in the process where Trello is useful. Arrange the bugs vertically in the backlog with the most important at the top, and the least important at the bottom.

The developer can then troubleshoot which issues are most important versus which will take the most time, and act accordingly. For example, if there's a bug at the bottom of the list, but it'll take thirty seconds to fix, the developer will make the quick changes and cross it off the list.

Just as in the beginning of the project, you should receive time estimates from your developer to determine how long each bug fix should take. Using Trello, you can continue to track progress like you would for any other milestone.

Sometimes you'll ship your product with bugs. Some bugs we call showstoppers; those are things that must be fixed in order to release the product. Most bugs are minor and people won't be too turned off by them.

Ultimately, it's up to the founder, their budget, and their timeline constraints to make a judgment call on whether a bug is detrimental to their product.

CHAPTER EIGHT CHECKLIST

- ☐ There is no such thing as a bug-free app.
- ☐ Be as specific and detailed as possible when reporting bugs to the developer.
- ☐ The founder is in charge of QA and testing the app for potential bugs.
- ☐ Don't blow the entire project budget on the first build.
- ☐ Provide a way for users to get in touch about issues.
- ☐ The founder decides whether a bug is detrimental to the product.

CONCLUSION

Congratulations! You've graduated to the final stage, and now you're ready to hire a developer and build your product!

If you followed the steps in this book, give yourself a pat on the back. You've successfully organized your mobile vision into a product spec, in turn saving yourself weeks of misspent time and tens of thousands of dollars in development costs. Great job!

Before we get to next steps, let me first acknowledge something—this book wouldn't be possible without Toptal. If Toptal didn't exist, I'd say you're screwed.

Hiring the right developer has traditionally been the

biggest hurdle for non-technical founders to overcome. Vetting the rock stars from the beginners requires deep technical expertise—running two- to three-hour technical interviews for each candidate, doing code reviews, programming tests, etc.

The two biggest newbie mistakes when outsourcing app development:

Presenting a risky, undefined project plan ✓ **Solved with Product Spec**

Hiring the wrong developer ✓ **Solved with Toptal**

Toptal ensures you only work with rock stars. They thoroughly vet every developer on their platform and only accept the top 3 percent of candidates who apply.[4] (That's two times more selective than Harvard!)

That means every developer they present to you is good. Top-of-their-field good. I call them 10xers.

The biggest thing I've learned outsourcing over one hundred apps is that working with top-notch developers is critical to the success of the project.

---

4   https://www.toptal.com/top-3-percent

10xers write better code and build products much faster than a newbie who's mediocre and slow. And because they're faster, they're also cheaper. The hourly rate might be two times higher than a newbie, but they finish the job four times faster.

Here's how Toptal works:

You create an account on Toptal.com and upload your project.

Toptal assigns you a sales engineer to understand your project needs and find candidates who would be a good fit.

You interview the candidates Toptal provides and hire the best candidate for your project.

Once hired, you begin a one-week trial with your candidate.

At the end of that first week, if you're not satisfied, you get 100 percent of your money back and restart the process. Otherwise, you continue working with the developer until the project is complete.

Once the project is complete, you either retain the developer and continue iterating together, or downshift to an hourly contract and return when you're ready for V.2.

It's essentially an on-demand developer service!

Now, for what everyone's been waiting for: As promised, through your completion of this book, you have earned a $1,000 Toptal credit for your project!

To claim your $1,000 Toptal credit, just create an account using the link toptal.com/#snag-just-top-coders-today and shoot me an email at drew@appfactorySF.com. I'll hook you up with the $1,000 credit and share some tips on how to run your interviews—including the top four interview questions to ask developers!

This might not be the closing sentiment you were expecting, but in all honesty, this is the best piece of advice I can provide before sending you into the wild world of app creation.

The app-building process is infinite. You will go through this process over and over again. Rinse, wash, repeat. Once you launch the app, talk to your users, gather feedback, and use this information to re-examine everything you've done. The user stories, for example: Are all the assumptions that you made about your users correct? Find what you were wrong about and rebuild that segment.

The realigned user stories can be used to re-evaluate the

wireframes and design new features, which can then be added to the product spec. Repeat this process until you find that product market fit, and are ready to scale up.

Scaling comes with a whole set of other challenges that are beyond the scope of this book, but, to get to that point, rinse, wash, repeat.

Want to tell me what you think of the book? Drop me a line at drew@appfactorysf.com or find me on Twitter @ drewgorham.

APPENDIX

HIRING A GRAPHIC DESIGNER

Hiring a graphic designer is a completely optional step, and not all products need a designer. As I mentioned with the user adoption curve, your first hundred users are not going to be the late majority who only sign up for an app once it's trending.

Early adopters are a cutting-edge range of people who tend to love a product for what it does, not how it looks, which is why hiring a graphic designer is not a necessity in the early stages. If your wireframes are good enough and you work with a talented developer, they should be able to make the app functional from the wireframes.

If you choose not to work with a graphic designer, the developer will implement the wireframes and recreate the interface you designed, or they might create their own UI design. There are certain developers out there who are what we refer to as "unicorns"—sounds magical, doesn't it? These are basically developers who also have design skills.

These "unicorn" developers can create a beautiful user interface without needing a designer, but like the mystical unicorn creature, this type of developer is rare. If you work with your average, run-of-the-mill developer, you can expect the app design to be rudimentary and not generally appealing.

All founders tend to let their ego get in the way of design decisions. This isn't a negative observation; it's instinctual to want your product to be as beautiful as possible, but this comes with a hefty price tag that many first-time founders don't have the budget for.

Not feeling confident in the app design can be a very real source of frustration. It's extremely difficult for founders to let go of design and let the app be ugly, but the primary concern when deciding whether or not to hire a designer is determining if your users actually care about the app's appearance. Perhaps they simply care about functionality, in which case a rudimentary design is fine; however, if they want a polished and finished product, you will need a designer to take the wireframes from rudimentary to beautiful.

Although this chapter is positioned after the discussion about hiring a developer, if you choose to work with a designer, I suggest doing so before the development phase. This allows you to present a completed product spec to your developer, and they won't have to wait on any additional design assets to do their job. (Note: post-design, you will need to circle back to the product spec and replace the wireframe screenshots with the actual designed screens.)

THE HIRING PROCESS

We know the reasons non-technical people are unqualified to hire developers, but hiring a designer requires a visual assessment, which is definitely in the realm of a non-tech founder. The language of designers is accessible, so you should be able to gauge their skills effectively and communicate with them in an interview.

To prepare your search for a designer, I recommend creating a mood board of visuals that inspire you. You can do this in a Google Doc and include screenshots from other apps, photographs that resonate with the design you have in mind, appealing app icons, logos you find attractive, and so forth. In conjunction with the wireframes, this visual content will be helpful for the designer to pull inspiration from.

KEY HIRING ELEMENTS

Most people are tempted to base their judgment entirely on a designer's portfolio, but in my experience communication is equally, if not more, important.

Working with any kind of freelancer on a remote basis, communication is key. A talented designer who doesn't communicate well is more hassle than they're worth. Similar to the expectations of your developer, a designer should keep you updated on estimated delivery dates and be responsive to your inquiries and needs.

When you combine a great portfolio with excellent communication skills, you've found the ideal designer.

TopTal can also connect you with vetted and skilled designers on their platform. The process is similar to hiring a developer: they create a job description for your project that reviews the kind of designer you're looking for and connect you with potential candidates who meet the criteria you've established.

Again, just as with their developers, TopTal only accepts the most elite designers, so the professionals they suggest will not only be talented, but they'll also be communicative, friendly, and helpful.

Once TopTal has connected you with potential candidates, you can schedule interviews to gauge their communication skills and project compatibility. Have them provide time estimates, and ask them specific questions to examine their communication style:

When I send you an e-mail, how long should I expect before I hear back?

What does your typical workday look like?

Are you available over Skype throughout the process to discuss revisions or time estimates?

Just like developers, each designer sets their own price, but they typically work for an hourly rate versus a weekly one. There's a wide range of prices; again, the disparity generally has more to do with cost of living than skill level.

Someone in the United States might charge $200 per hour, but someone in Malaysia might charge $30 per hour for the same quality of work. Again, it's counterintuitive that these two price points could produce the same caliber of work, but the global outsourcing movement has made it possible.

The average price point for a talented designer should be in the $50-60 per hour range, and although there are many different variables that could affect the timeline, allotting about an hour of design work for each screen is a reasonable estimate.

WATCH OUT FOR THE PITFALLS!

When hiring a designer, there are a few things to keep in mind. Aside from seeking designers with impressive portfolios who seem responsive and communicative, you'll also want to:

- Hire someone who understands your vision and can be objective about the app.
- Make sure the designer is curious about understanding the potential user they're designing for.
- Avoid crowd design sites like CrowdStreams and 99Designs. Sites such as these generally offer to design a variety of logos for $200, which seems like a great deal, but I've had experiences where the logos are actually rip-offs from other companies. This is a blatant trademark violation, and, go figure, the support staff from these companies seem to

disappear post-delivery. Sometimes if something sounds too good to be true, it is.

WORKING WITH A DESIGNER

When I work with designers, I encourage them to exercise creative freedom. The wireframes are just one version of how the app could flow, and the designer might be able to provide creative insight into the structure of the app.

The wireframes shouldn't be a rigid guide for the app's UI design; they are simply the visual way of demonstrating the functional requirements of the app. As long as the functionality remains intact, I give designers the freedom to offer creative and visually engaging alternatives to my initial designs.

Once you hire a designer, you want to monitor the look and feel of the designs as they're being produced. Request the designer work on one or two screens at a time, then have them submit them to you for review so you can provide feedback.

The feedback loop is much more effective than having all the screens designed at once and not seeing the progress until the end results are delivered. Without the feedback loop, the workflow results in a lot of unnecessary work 99 percent of the time, and since most designers are paid on an hourly basis, it will cost you more money.

Through TopTal, designers have a one-week trial period, so it's especially important that you review their initial designs within the first week to ensure they're a good fit.

Once the designs are completed and the product moves into development stage, it's best to stay in touch with the designer in case the developer needs additional assets or there's a need to alter a design. Having the designer on tap will hopefully prevent any significant delays in the development phase.

APPENDIX CHECKLIST

- ☐ Hiring a designer is an optional step.
- ☐ A designer will take the rudimentary wireframes and make a visually appealing UI.
- ☐ Non-technical people are qualified to conduct comprehensive design interviews.
- ☐ Designers should be evaluated on portfolio and communication style.
- ☐ Create a mood board that depicts the app's visual feel.
- ☐ Request regular updates from the designer, both verbal and visual.
- ☐ Give the designer creative freedom during the design process.

ACKNOWLEDGMENTS

———

Famed computer scientist Donald Knuth once said, "Premature optimization is the root of all evil." It's one of the easiest quotes to appreciate and one of the hardest to follow.

Walking the fine line between too much information and just enough information has been the greatest challenge with this project. Thankfully, I've been fortunate to be surrounded by a cast of support throughout the journey.

First, I want to thank my wife Marie-Clare. Without her, I'd be dithering away in a Philosophy Ph.D. program, probably growing a beard (badly) and writing a much less useful book.

Next, thanks to my father, Chris, my mother, Cheryl, and

Carl and Robin Treseder. You guys were my angel investors. I couldn't have done this without your support.

To my favorite App Factory customer, JP Vasellina, for sitting me down for coffee one day and telling me to write down this methodology and share it with other aspiring entrepreneurs. This was all JP's idea.

Many thanks to the Book in a Box team: Zach Obront, Mark Chait, Justine Schofield, Sheila Trask, and Dan Bernitt for pushing me through to the finish line.

And finally, thank you to all the hundreds of non-technical entrepreneurs who worked these ideas out with me. Without your faith in me, we never would have taken the risks and run the experiments to discover this methodology.

ABOUT THE AUTHOR

 **DREW GORHAM**, founder of App Factory, is an award-winning product manager who has coached hundreds of non-technical entrepreneurs through the early stages of product development. He now works with national security government organizations to apply the lean product development approach toward solving national security problems.

During the summer, Drew teaches a leading innovation program at Stanford University, the Silicon Valley Innovation Academy.

Best known for cultivating offshore technical teams for rapid MVP development, Drew has designed and developed over one hundred apps since 2013.

Prior to founding App Factory, Drew was a developer and technical project manager, building apps for Fortune 500 companies including Intel, Tesla Motors, and Kaiser Permanente.

70042120R10076

Made in the USA
Middletown, DE
25 September 2019